LEGO friends

Perfect Pets

Written by Lisa Stock

LONDON, NEW YORK, MUNICH,
MELBOURNE and DELHI

DK LONDON
Editor Lisa Stock
Designer Toby Truphet
Pre-Production Producer Siu Yin Chan
Producer Louise Minihane
Managing Editor Elizabeth Dowsett
Design Manager Ron Stobbart
Publishing Manager Julie Ferris
Publishing Director Simon Beecroft

DK DELHI
Assistant Editor Gaurav Joshi
Assistant Art Editor Pranika Jain
Art Editor Divya Jain
Deputy Managing Editor Chitra Subramanyam
Deputy Managing Art Editor Neha Ahuja
DTP Designer Umesh Singh Rawat
Senior DTP Designer Jagtar Singh
Pre Production Manager Sunil Sharma

Reading Consultant
Maureen Fernandes

First published in Great Britain by
Dorling Kindersley Limited
80 Strand, London, WC2R 0RL

10 9 8 7 6 5 4 3 2 1
001–196549–May/14

Colour reproduction by Alta Image
Printed and bound in China by South China

Discover more at
www.dk.com
www.LEGO.com

Contents

4   Welcome to Heartlake City

6   Jazz

8   Scarlett

10   Caring for Pets

12   Cotton

14   Dear Nicole

16   Felix and Max

18   Ruby

20   Heartlake City News

22   Lady

24   Heartlake Pet Salon

26   Daisy

28   Bella

30   At the Vet

32   On the Ranch

34   Busy Workers

36   Maxie and Goldie

38   Looking After Zobo

40   Pet Gallery

42   Quiz

44   Glossary

45   Index

46   Guide for Parents

Welcome to Heartlake City

This is Mia.

Do you like animals?

Mia does!

This is her

dog Charlie.

Charlie sleeps in a cool kennel
that Mia helped to decorate.

Mia's friends Olivia, Emma,
Stephanie and Andrea all
love animals too.
The girls enjoy spending time
with all their pets.
Let's meet some of them.

Jazz

Jazz is Andrea's rabbit.
Andrea grows carrots for
her furry friend in her garden.

Cheeky Jazz makes quite a mess eating his carrots!
Andrea sets to work tidying the hutch with a broom.

Scarlett

Scarlett is Olivia's puppy.
Olivia and Mia train her
to perform in dog shows.

Scarlett also likes to run around playing football with Stephanie.

CARING FOR PETS

Looking after a pet is a very important job.
The friends try to follow these helpful tips:

Things to do...

✓ Do provide healthy food and clean, fresh water every day.

✓ Do make sure your pet has a nice, comfy place to sleep.

✓ Do make sure your pet gets plenty of exercise.

✓ Do give your pet lots of love and attention, and some treats!

Things not to do...

X Do not feed your pet human food.
Its own food is better for its stomach.

X Do not bath your pet too often.
Some pets do not need bathing at
all since they clean themselves.

X Do not leave your pet by itself
too much. It can get lonely.

X Do not forget
to take your
pet to the
vet for regular
check-ups.

Oscar visits the vet.

Cotton

Stephanie is looking after
a newborn lamb called Cotton.
Cotton has got very dirty
playing outside.
Stephanie gently washes her
woolly fleece.

Nicole

23, Maple Street,

Spring Town

Snow is so adorable!

405, River Street,
Heartlake City

12th June

Dear Nicole,

There is a new arrival at Heartlake Stables!
Snow is a white foal, born just two weeks ago.

It was very funny to watch Snow try to stand
up right away. She was very wobbly at first,
but she soon got the hang of it.

I visit Snow every morning and evening.
She is definitely starting to recognise me now.

I am sending you a picture of Snow so you
can see for yourself how sweet she is.

Lots of love,
Olivia

Felix and Max

Felix the cat likes to pounce and play on the playground the girls have built for him.

Max the puppy thinks it is much
more fun to climb up and down
the seesaw outside his playhouse.

Ruby

Ruby is Stephanie's horse.
They are entering a show-
jumping competition together.

They have been practising
for months!
Now Stephanie is sure that
Ruby is ready to compete.
Good luck you two!

HEARTLAKE CITY
NEWS

Ruby Jumps her Way to Victory!

Heartlake City Correspondent

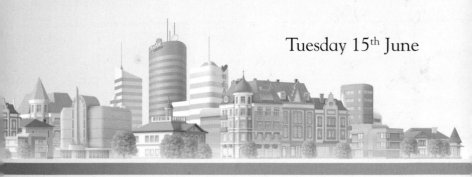

Hundreds of people came to watch the annual Heartlake City Horse Show yesterday. After some great riding, the top prize ribbon was awarded to Ruby and her owner Stephanie.

The pair displayed some wonderful skills, clearing all the jumps with ease. The audience loved them.

Stephanie told us, "We practised so much for this competition. Ruby is going to get lots of treats now!"

Let's hope they will be back again to compete next year.

HEARTLAKE Pet Salon

VOUCHER
Bring your pet for a free grooming session and lots of pampering.

Lady

Lady the poodle is at
Heartlake Pet Salon.
She loves being washed in
the bath and having her
hair brushed and trimmed.

The salon has so
many accessories.
A crown is the perfect
choice for Lady.
Now she is ready for
a walk in the park.

HEARTLAKE
Pet Salon

Bubble bath

Shampoo

Accessories

Bow

Water dish

24

Hairbrush

Till

Hairdryer

8

Treats

Flowers

Bird house

Bone

25

Daisy

Daisy is Stephanie's bunny.
She has learnt how to perform
clever magic tricks with Mia.

Daisy also helps Stephanie look for lost animals on a cool patrol bike.

Bella

Bella is Mia's horse.
Mia makes sure Bella
is fit and well.

Once Mia took Bella to the vet because she had a stone stuck in her hoof.
Ouch!

AT THE VET

Today's Patients

Sophie the vet looks after all the sick animals at Heartlake City Vet Surgery.

First she finds out what is wrong with them.

Then she treats them to make them well again.

Name	Scarlett
Species	Dog
Weight	6kg
Diagnosis	Broken leg
Treatment	Cast on her leg and lots of rest

Name	Oscar
Species	Hedgehog
Weight	350g
Diagnosis	Eye infection
Treatment	Eye drops applied daily

Name	Major
Species	Horse
Weight	485kg
Diagnosis	Cough
Treatment	Medicine to soothe his throat

Name	Lucky
Species	Rabbit
Weight	2kg
Diagnosis	Thorn stuck in paw
Treatment	Thorn removed and special cream applied

On the Ranch

Mia works on her grandparents' ranch with her friend Liza.

Horses, rabbits, cats and hens
live on Sunshine Ranch,
so it is very busy and noisy.

After a long horse ride,
Liza and Mia rest under a
beautiful tree on the ranch.

Busy Workers

There are many jobs to
do on the ranch.
Liza loves feeding carrots
to the rabbits.

Mia collects eggs that
Clara the hen has laid.
The eggs will make
a delicious lunch!

Maxie and Goldie

The girls look after Maxie
the cat in their club tree house.
The friends also take
care of Goldie the bird.
When he broke his
wing, they built him
a bird box to
recover in.

Looking After Zobo

Olivia has built a robot called Zobo. He is not an animal, but he still makes a great pet. However, looking after a robot is quite different from a normal pet.

Chalkboard

Olivia carefully writes all of Zobo's programming on the blackboard.

Remote control

A handy remote control directs Zobo's every move.

Binoculars

Zobo's lenses must be kept clean so that he can see.

Batteries
Zobo's batteries need to be charged every night.

Tools
Power tools keep Zobo's parts tightly screwed.

Oil Can
Regular oiling keeps Zobo's parts working properly.

39

PET GALLERY

This photo album belongs to .....Mia.....

Emma makes sure that Lady looks her best before going for a walk.

Olivia does not mind getting wet with Maxie in the tub.

Scrubbing a large horse like Bella is never easy.

When no one is around, Stephanie likes talking to Cotton for hours.

Andrea works hard so Jazz has a clean and comfy hutch to sleep in.

Quiz

1. Who does Jazz belong to?

2. What is the name of the newborn lamb?

3. Which pet has a seesaw outside his playhouse?

4. Which pet enters a show-jumping competition?

5. Where does Lady go to get her hair trimmed?

6. Which pet performs magic tricks with Mia?

7. Which pet once got a stone stuck in her hoof?

8. Who loves feeding carrots to rabbits on Sunshine Ranch?

9. Where do the girls look after Maxie the cat?

10. What did Goldie the bird break?

Answers on
page 45

Glossary

accessories
extra items that
can be worn

diagnosis
nature of
an illness

foal
baby horse

groom
brush and clean an
animal's coat

kennel
shelter for a dog

microscope
machine that makes
very small objects look
larger so they can be
seen in more detail

ranch
large farm where
lots of animals
live together

recognise
to find someone or
something familiar

remote control
mechanical device
that controls
something from
a distance

stray
animal that does not
have a home

vet
doctor for animals

Index

Andrea 5, 6, 7, 41

Bella 28–29, 41

Charlie 4, 5
Clara 35
Cotton 12, 41

Daisy 26–27

Emma 5, 40

Felix 16

Goldie 36

Heartlake City Horse
 Show 21
Heartlake Pet Salon 21,
 22, 24–25

Jazz 6–7, 41

Lady 22–23, 40
Liza 32, 33, 34

Max 17
Maxie 36, 40
Mia 4, 5, 8, 26, 28, 29
 32, 33, 35, 40

Nicole 14, 15

Olivia 5, 8, 15, 38, 40
Oscar 11, 31

Ruby 18–19, 20, 21

Scarlett 8–9, 30
Snow 14, 15

Stephanie 5, 9, 12, 18,
 19, 21, 26, 27, 41
Sunshine Ranch 7, 27

vet 11, 29, 30

Zobo 38–39

Answers to the quiz on pages 42 and 43:
1. Andrea 2. Cotton 3. Max the puppy
4. Ruby 5. To Heartlake Pet Salon 6. Daisy
7. Bella 8. Liza 9. In their club tree house
10. His wing

Guide for Parents

DK Reads is a three-level reading series for children, developing the habit of reading widely for both pleasure and information. These books have exciting running text interspersed with a range of reading genres to suit your child's reading ability, as required by the school curriculum. Each book is designed to develop your child's reading skills, fluency, grammar awareness and comprehension in order to build confidence and engagement when reading.

Ready for a *Beginning to Read* book
YOUR CHILD SHOULD

- be using phonics, including combinations of consonants, such as bl, gl and sm, to read unfamiliar words; and common word endings, such as plurals, ing, ed and ly.
- be using the storyline, illustrations and the grammar of a sentence to check and correct their own reading.
- be pausing briefly at commas, and for longer at full stops; and altering his/her expression to respond to question, exclamation and speech marks.

A Valuable And Shared Reading Experience

For many children, reading requires much effort but adult participation can make this both fun and easier. So here are a few tips on how to use this book with your child.

TIP 1: Check out the contents together before your child begins:

- Read the text about the book on the back cover.
- Read through and discuss the contents page together to heighten your child's interest and expectation.
- Briefly discuss any unfamiliar or difficult words on the contents page.

- Chat about the non-fiction reading features used in the book, such as headings, captions, recipes, lists or charts.

This introduction helps to put your child in control and makes the reading challenge less daunting.

TIP 2: Support your child as he/she reads the story pages:

- Give the book to your child to read and turn the pages.
- Where necessary, encourage your child to break a word into syllables, sound out each one and then flow the syllables together. Ask him/her to reread the sentence to check the meaning.
- When there's a question mark or an exclamation mark, encourage your child to vary his/her voice as he/she reads the sentence. Demonstrate how to do this if it is helpful.

TIP 3: Praise, share and chat:

- The factual pages tend to be more difficult than the story pages, and are designed to be shared with your child.
- Ask questions about the text and the meaning of the words used. Ask your child to suggest his/her own quiz questions. These help to develop comprehension skills and awareness of the language used.

A FEW ADDITIONAL TIPS

- Try and read together every day. Little and often is best. After 10 minutes, only keep going if your child wants to read on.
- Always encourage your child to have a go at reading difficult words by themselves. Praise any self-corrections, for example, "I like the way you sounded out that word and then changed the way you said it, to make sense."
- Read other books of different types to your child just for enjoyment and information.

Here are some other DK Reads you might enjoy.

Beginning to Read

Pirate Attack!
Come and join Captain Blackbeard and his pirate crew for an action-packed adventure on the high seas.

Deadly Dinosaurs
Roar! Thud! Meet Roxy, Sid, Deano and Sonia, the museum dinosaurs that come alive at night.

LEGO® Legends of Chima™: Tribes of Chima
Friend or Foe? Meet the amazing animal tribes of Chima and discover their fearsome vehicles and weapons.

Playful Puppy
Holly's life almost changes when the new playful puppy comes home one fine day.

Starting to Read Alone

The Great Panda Tale
Join the excitement at the zoo as the staff prepare to welcome a new panda baby.

LEGO® Friends: Summer Adventures
Emjoy a summer of fun in Heartlake City with Emma, Mia, Andrea Stephanie, Olivia and friends.

LEGO® Legends of Chima™: Heroes' Quest
Come and join the band of heroes as they set out to find the Legend Beasts and save Chima from a crisis.